HAL LEONARD

VENOVA™ METHOD

CONTENTS

This book is based on *Venova for Beginners* by Yamaha Music Entertainment Holdings, Inc.

To access video visit:
www.halleonard.com/mylibrary

Enter Code
3085-5712-0380-0739

ISBN 978-1-5400-6413-4

HAL•LEONARD®

© 2018 Yamaha Music Entertainment Holdings, Inc.
This edition published 2020 by Hal Leonard LLC

Visit Hal Leonard Online at
www.halleonard.com

Contact us:
Hal Leonard
7777 West Bluemound Road
Milwaukee, WI 53213
Email: info@halleonard.com

In Europe, contact:
Hal Leonard Europe Limited
42 Wigmore Street
Marylebone, London, W1U 2RN
Email: info@halleonardeurope.com

In Australia, contact:
Hal Leonard Australia Pty. Ltd.
4 Lentara Court
Cheltenham, Victoria, 3192 Australia
Email: info@halleonard.com.au

INTRODUCTION

The Venova* is a new type of wind instrument that was invented to provide as many people as possible with an opportunity to enjoy wind instruments more easily and freely. With its simple, recorder-like fingering, you can enjoy playing music expressively, just like with a saxophone.

Light, durable and easy to maintain, the Venova can be enjoyed casually in a variety of situations such as outdoor events and music sessions.

The name "Venova" is derived from the Latin words *ventus* and *nova*, meaning "wind" and "new" respectively.

A variety of instructional videos are available at **www.halleonard.com/mylibrary**. They provide additional information such as instrument set-up, how to make sound, practice pieces and a selection of songs. These videos offer helpful guidance, especially for beginners. Simply enter the code from page 1 of this book to access all the videos for download or streaming.

Why not take this opportunity to experience the enjoyment of playing a wind instrument!

*Venova is a registered trademark of the Yamaha Corporation.

NOMENCLATURE

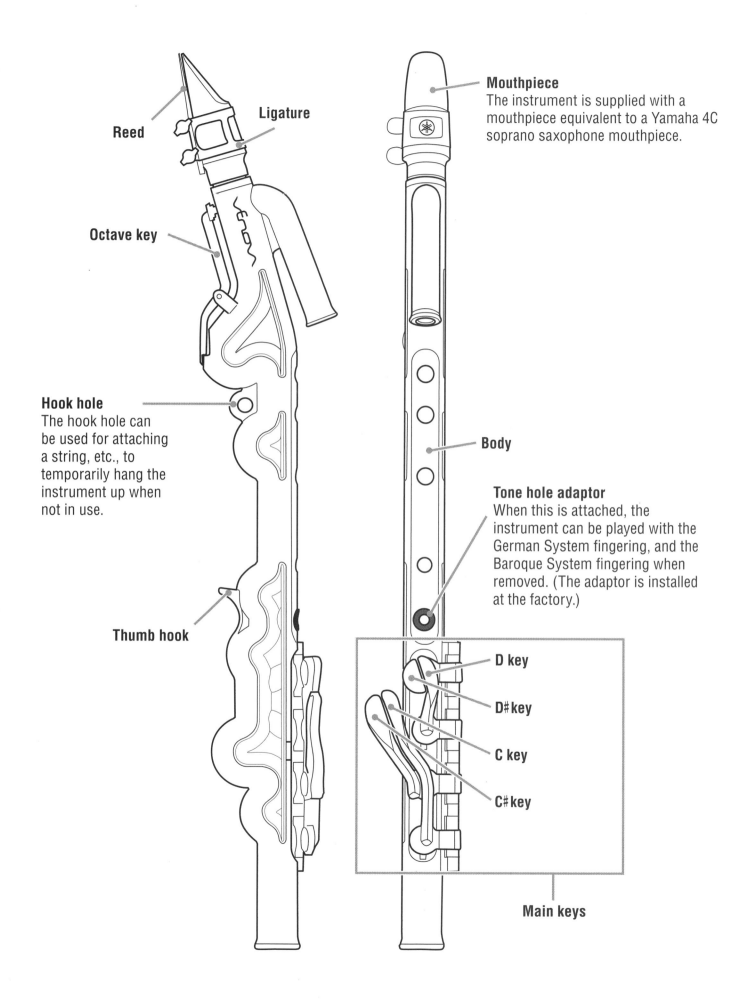

Reed

Ligature

Octave key

Hook hole
The hook hole can be used for attaching a string, etc., to temporarily hang the instrument up when not in use.

Thumb hook

Mouthpiece
The instrument is supplied with a mouthpiece equivalent to a Yamaha 4C soprano saxophone mouthpiece.

Body

Tone hole adaptor
When this is attached, the instrument can be played with the German System fingering, and the Baroque System fingering when removed. (The adaptor is installed at the factory.)

D key

D♯ key

C key

C♯ key

Main keys

SETTING UP THE INSTRUMENT

 Let's Play the Venova! 1) Setting the Reed and Ligature

SETTING THE REED AND LIGATURE

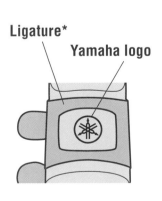

1. Grasp the mouthpiece firmly, and slide it onto the neck joint of the body, twisting back and forth.

   Use the same twisting action when removing the mouthpiece, as attaching or pulling the mouthpiece straight off could result in damage to the rubber of the neck joint.

2. Slide the ligature onto the mouthpiece from its tapered end.

3. If you are using a reed made from cane, rather than the resin reed supplied with the instrument, moisten the end of the reed in your mouth (or with water) before playing.

4. Attach the reed onto the mouthpiece. First, place the reed so that the top edge of the mouthpiece is visible over the end of the reed, and then tighten the two ligature screws to secure the reed.

ABOUT THE REED

The reed tip is delicate so take care not to damage it with the ligature, etc.

Replace the supplied reed with a new one if the tip becomes damaged or if it no longer vibrates well.

In addition to the resin reed, soprano saxophone reeds made of cane can also be used.

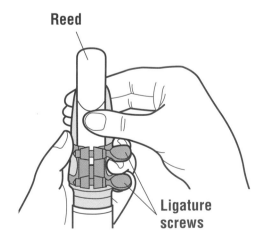

Reed

Ligature screws

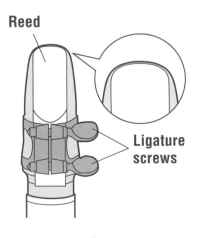

Reed

Ligature screws

Ligature*

Yamaha logo

*Position the ligature so that the Yamaha logo is centered in the ligature's open space.

HOLDING THE INSTRUMENT

FINGER POSITION

Use the pad of your finger (not the tip) to cover the hole.

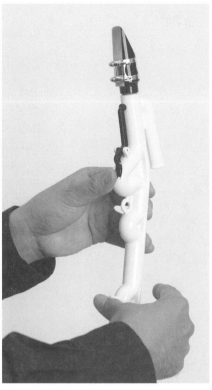

Octave Key
The octave key is used for playing notes above a high D. It is not used for playing any other notes, so take care not to press the octave key by mistake.

Place your right thumb under the thumb hook to hold the instrument securely.

LAYING THE INSTRUMENT DOWN

When the instrument is not being played, place it on a flat surface as shown in the pictures on the right. Do not place the instrument on a chair, music stand, or other unstable surface, where it may fall. Also, never lean the instrument up against a wall, etc.

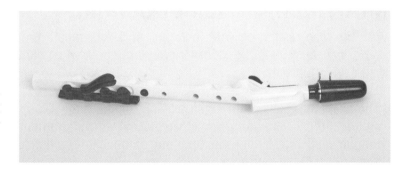

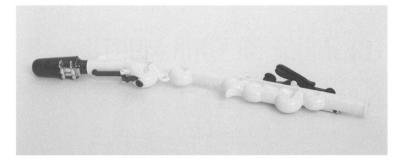

MAKING SOUNDS

 Let's Play the Venova! 2) Tips on Making Sound

 Let's Play the Venova! 3) Blowing the Instrument

1. Hold the instrument as shown in the picture below, keeping your back straight, shoulders relaxed, and chin tucked.

2. Position the mouthpiece in your mouth with your upper front teeth resting about 1cm from the tip of the mouthpiece. Cover your lower teeth with your lower lip to keep your teeth from coming into direct contact with the reed.

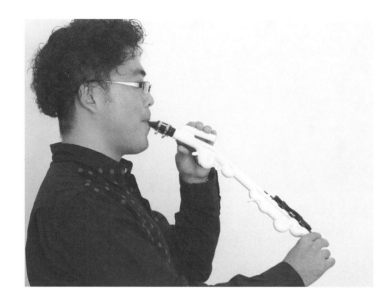

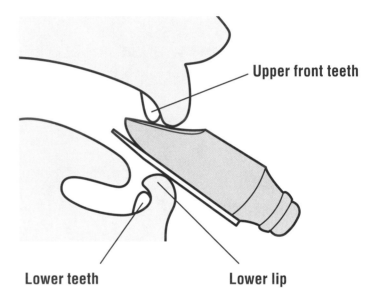

Upper front teeth

Lower teeth   **Lower lip**

MOUTH SHAPE (EMBOUCHURE*)

With the reed resting on your lower lip, seal your mouth around the mouthpiece to keep air from escaping out of the corners of your mouth when blowing. Do not bite hard on the reed or mouthpiece.

*The shape of your mouth when playing the instrument is called the "embouchure." The embouchure is very important when playing wind instruments. Proper positioning of lips, tongue, teeth, etc., creates an optimum embouchure, which allows you to control the pitch and timbre of the instrument.

THE INSIDE OF YOUR MOUTH

When blowing into the instrument, the inside of your mouth should be shaped as if you were pronouncing "OH."

Take a deep breath and blow into the instrument.

Compared to a recorder, the Venova requires more breath to play. Use a lot of air and blow firmly into the instrument.

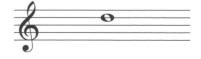

The sound produced is close to the note D.

HOW TO PLAY THE NOTE G

 Let's Play the Venova! 4) Fingering of G

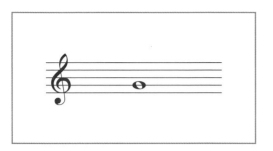

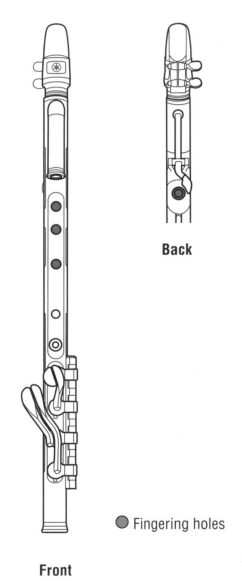

Back

🔘 Fingering holes

Front

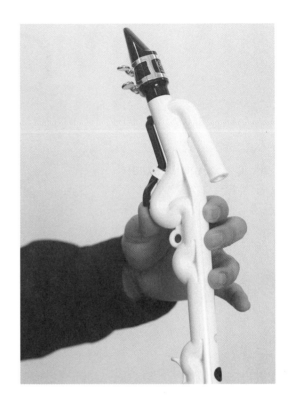

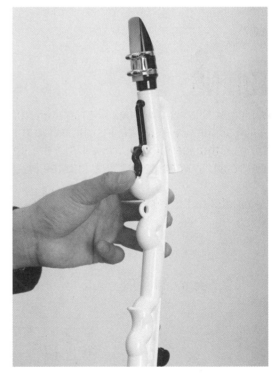

ABDOMINAL BREATHING

The breathing technique for the Venova is the same as natural abdominal breathing during sleep.

If you lay on your back and place your hand on your belly, can you feel your belly expand as you breathe? Try to visualize and mimic this breathing action while standing.

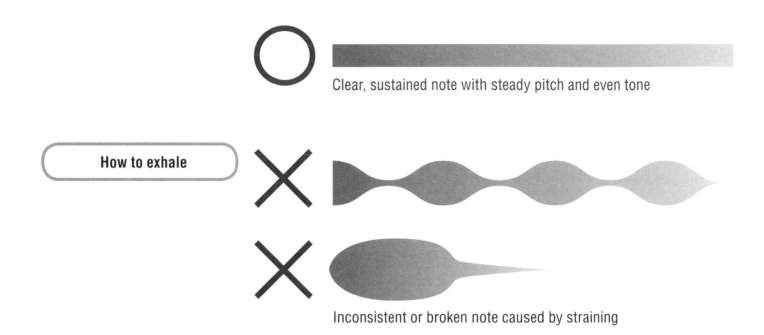

Clear, sustained note with steady pitch and even tone

How to exhale

Inconsistent or broken note caused by straining

TUNING

Basically, the Venova does not require tuning. The instrument is designed to play tuned to A=442Hz when the mouthpiece is slid all the way onto the instrument. If the instrument needs to be tuned to another pitch, it can be tuned lower by pulling the mouthpiece slightly away from the body. Since the temperature of the inside of the instrument affects the tuning (particularly when cold), blow into the instrument to warm it before tuning it.

Be careful not to pull the mouthpiece too far out. Pulling too far can result in poor intonation, making it hard to play.

Slide mouthpiece out to lower the pitch

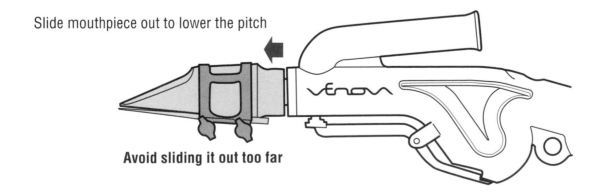

Avoid sliding it out too far

GETTING A BALANCED SOUND

If you are experiencing difficulty getting sound from your instrument, it might be good to review your embouchure.

Mouth shape and teeth alignment vary greatly among individuals, so take time to find the embouchure that works best for you. Refer to the chart below and try varying the position of your teeth and the angle that you hold the instrument, etc., to find a well-balanced tone.

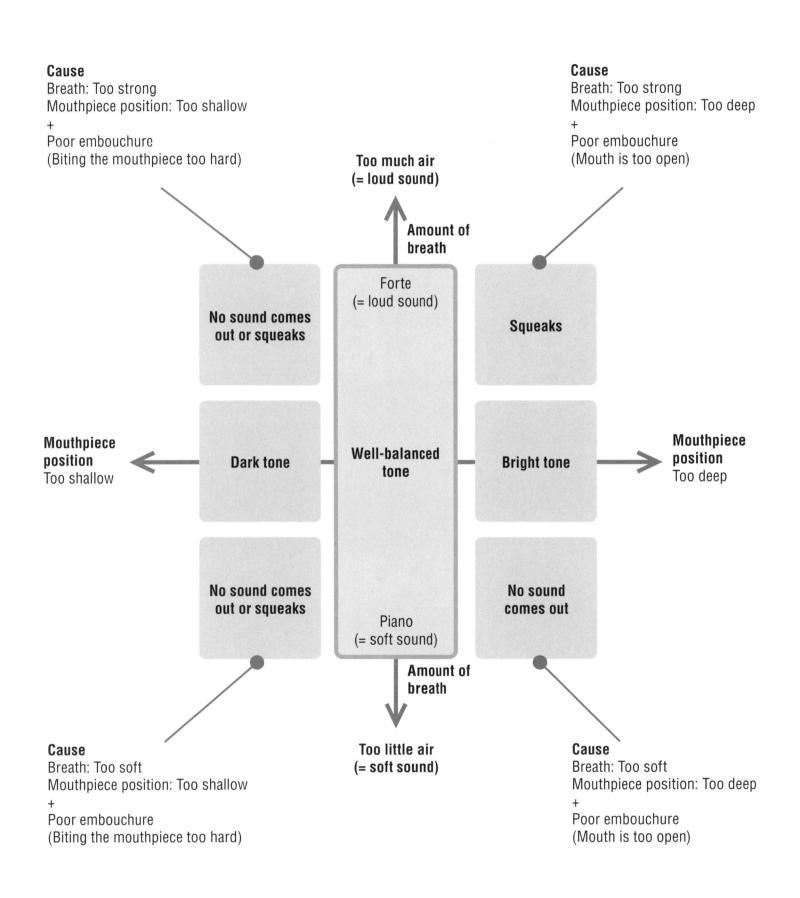

Cause
Breath: Too strong
Mouthpiece position: Too shallow
+
Poor embouchure
(Biting the mouthpiece too hard)

Cause
Breath: Too strong
Mouthpiece position: Too deep
+
Poor embouchure
(Mouth is too open)

**Too much air
(= loud sound)**

Amount of breath

Forte
(= loud sound)

No sound comes out or squeaks

Squeaks

Mouthpiece position
Too shallow

Dark tone

Well-balanced tone

Bright tone

Mouthpiece position
Too deep

No sound comes out or squeaks

Piano
(= soft sound)

No sound comes out

Amount of breath

**Too little air
(= soft sound)**

Cause
Breath: Too soft
Mouthpiece position: Too shallow
+
Poor embouchure
(Biting the mouthpiece too hard)

Cause
Breath: Too soft
Mouthpiece position: Too deep
+
Poor embouchure
(Mouth is too open)

TONGUING TECHNIQUE

Tonguing is a technique for dividing a tone by interrupting the air flow with your tongue.

The basic tonguing (or mouth shape) is "Toh."

Touch the reed with the tip of your tongue while breathing. This stops the vibration of the reed and subsequently mutes the sound. When you release your tongue from the reed, the reed then vibrates and sound is made. This is the tonguing technique. To begin, let's play with the mouth shape (or pronunciation) of the sound "Toh."

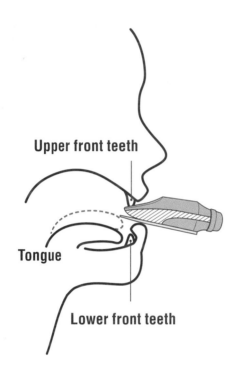

Upper front teeth

Tongue

Lower front teeth

✘ **Incorrect Technique**

Don't place too much of your tongue on the reed.

Are you placing your tongue too heavily on the reed? This will prevent you from breathing and will make the attack of the note slower. Be sure you use just the tip of your tongue on the reed, and only touch the reed when breathing.

LET'S PRACTICE

While breathing, touch the tip of your tongue to the reed.

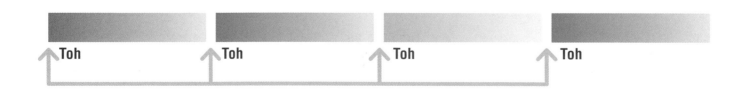

↑Toh   ↑Toh   ↑Toh   ↑Toh

TONGUING PRACTICE

1. Let's practice playing the note A.

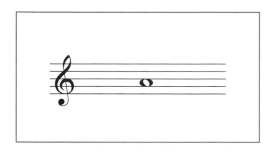

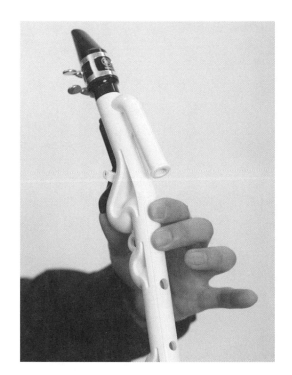

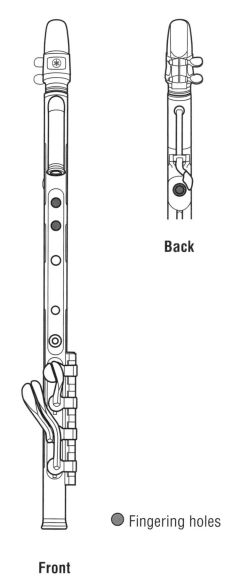

Back

● Fingering holes

Front

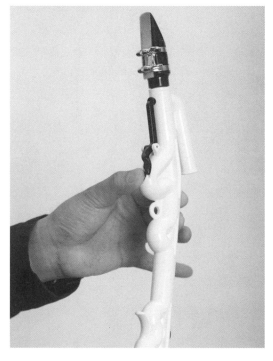

 Tonguing Practice: Let's practice playing the note A.

2. Let's practice playing the note B.

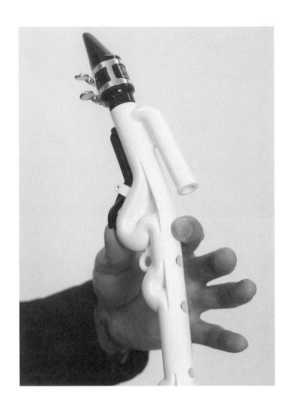

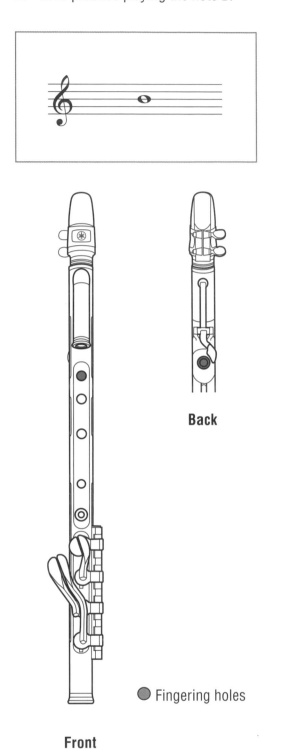

Back

● Fingering holes

Front

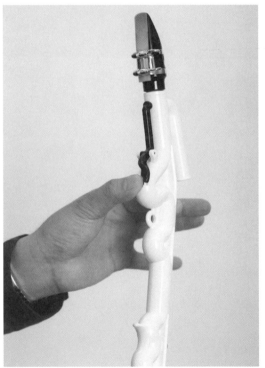

♩=100

PLAYING WITH DYNAMICS

1. Let's practice playing the note C.

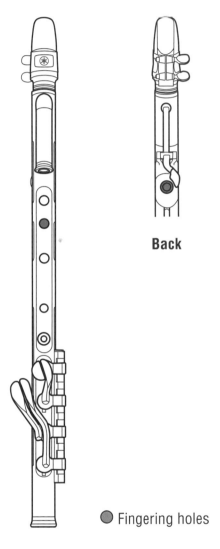

Back

⬤ Fingering holes

Front

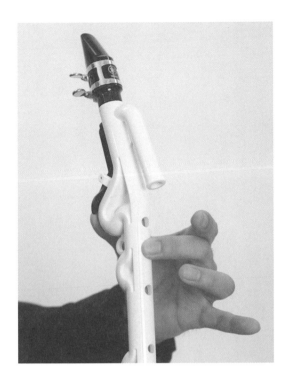

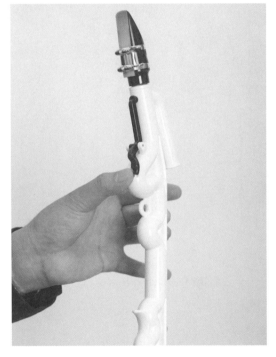

 Playing with Dynamics: Let's practice playing the note C.

2. Let's practice playing the note D.

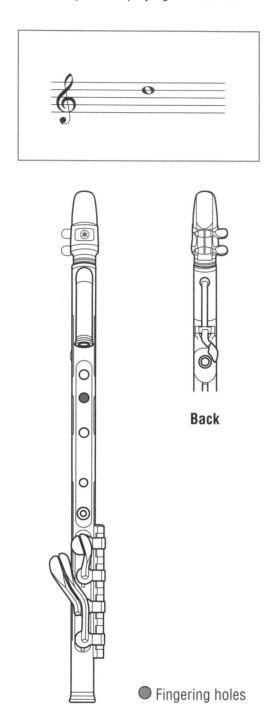

Back

🔴 Fingering holes

Front

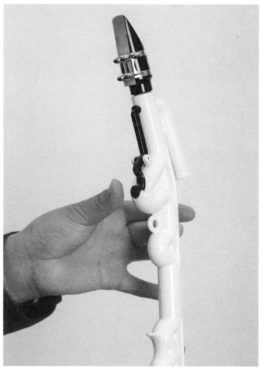

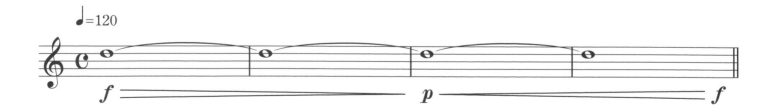

LET'S PLAY: "WHEN THE SAINTS GO MARCHING IN"

You can now play "When the Saints Go Marching In" with the five notes you have just learned: G, A, B, C and D!

 Let's Play the Venova! 5) Fingering of G, A, B, C and D

 Let's Play the Venova! 6) "When the Saints Go Marching In"

WHEN THE SAINTS GO MARCHING IN

Traditional

ADDING ARTICULATIONS

STACCATO

To add staccato notes, we can use the pronunciation of the sounds "Tuh" or "Tah" which are shorter than the sound of "Toh."

 Adding Articulations, Staccato

SLUR

A slur is an articulation used when you want to play smoothly across two or more different-pitched notes. To play a slur, tongue the first note as normal, but don't tongue the following notes in the group.

 Adding Articulations, Slur

VIBRATO

conceptual diagram

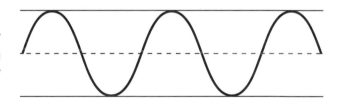

Vibrato is an articulation which enhances the beauty of the tone by adding a wavy vibration to the sound, without altering the pitch. To add vibrato, alter the embouchure (mouthing of the instrument) by tensing and relaxing the lips and jaw repeatedly.

The following shows the speed of the vibrato waves as a rhythm pattern. Let's practice with a tempo of 72 BPM. The speed of the 16th-note rhythm in the 4th bar creates a beautiful-sounding vibrato.

 Adding Articulations, Vibrato

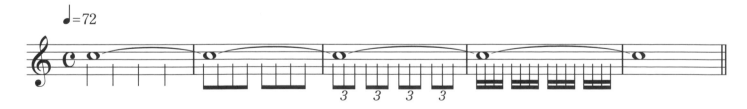

LET'S PLAY: "AMAZING GRACE"

Learn two more notes, and you can play "Amazing Grace"!

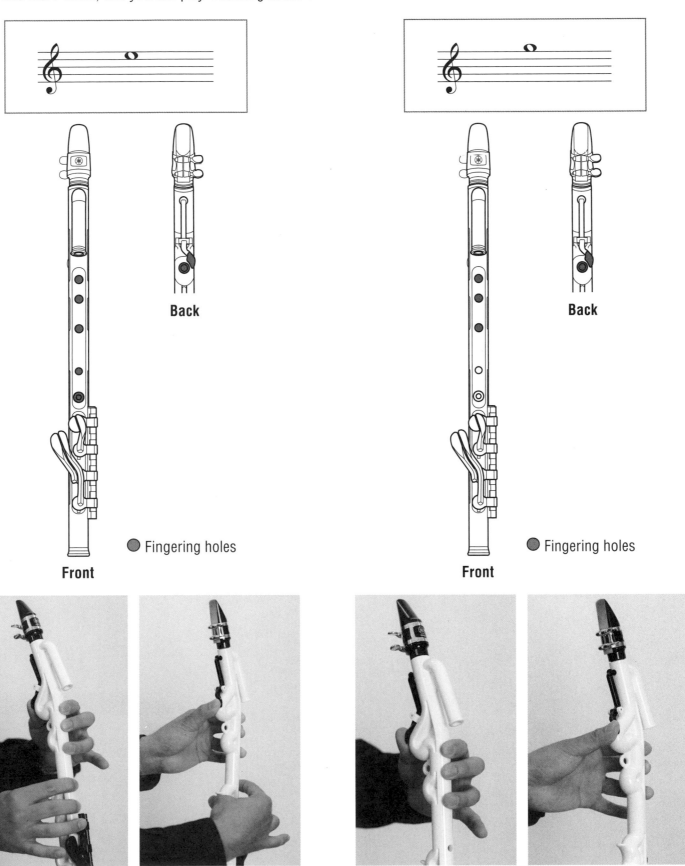

Back

Back

🔴 Fingering holes

🔴 Fingering holes

Front

Front

 Let's play the Venova! 7) Fingering of High E, F and G Using the Octave Key

AMAZING GRACE

Words by John Newton
From A Collection of Sacred Ballads
Traditional American Melody
From Carrell and Clayton's Virginia Harmony
Arranged by Edwin O. Excell

 Let's Play the Venova! 8) "Amazing Grace"

INSTRUMENT MAINTENANCE

After playing, always loosen the ligature, remove the reed from the mouthpiece and then wipe dry with a clean cloth. Remove the ligature from the mouthpiece.

Take care to avoid damaging the end of the mouthpiece.

Remove the mouthpiece from the instrument and clean the inside of the mouthpiece with a soft cloth. Clean the inside of the instrument with the supplied cleaning swab.

Twist and pull the mouthpiece from side to side when removing it.

Attaching or detaching the mouthpiece without twisting could result in damage to the rubber of the neck joint.

 Instrument Maintenance (Using the Cleaning Swab)

USING THE CLEANING SWAB

1. Insert the end of the swab's ball chain into the body from the neck joint of the instrument.

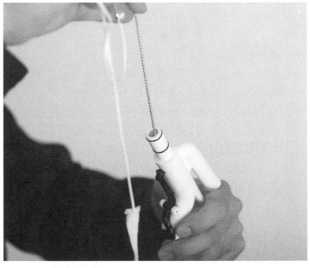

2. Gently shake the instrument so that the ball chain comes out of the opposite end.

3. Pull on the ball chain gently so that the cleaning swab can remove moisture and dirt from the inside of the body.

Pulling the cleaning swab too fast can result in the swab becoming stuck in the body.

Always keep the cleaning swab clean and dry.

Use a soft cloth to wipe the instrument's surface. Avoid applying excessive force on the keys.

Both the mouthpiece and body are washable. After washing, use a cleaning swab or a soft cloth to thoroughly remove moisture.

PLACING THE INSTRUMENT IN THE CASE

When placing the instrument in the case, make sure that the mouthpiece is aligned correctly with the body. Make sure that the mouthpiece is properly attached to avoid the possibility of damage to the instrument.

The slide locks on the case lid (A) slightly protrude from the case. Be sure that your clothing or the cleaning swab do not get caught on either of the locks causing the case or instrument to fall.

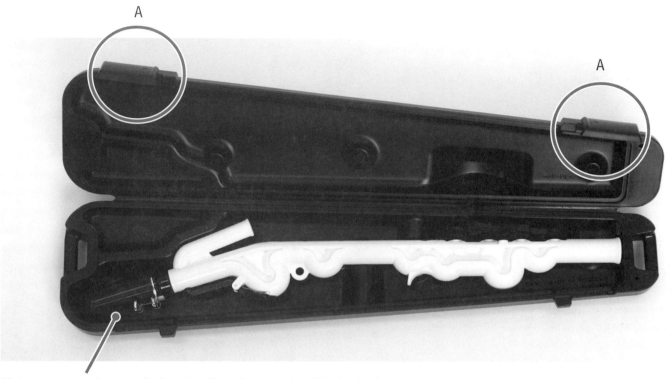

Make sure that the mouthpiece is aligned correctly with the body.

Difficulty Level

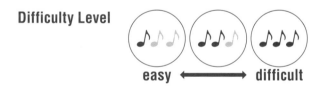

easy ⟷ difficult

HAPPY BIRTHDAY TO YOU

Words and Music by Mildred J. Hill and Patty S. Hill

FURUSATO

Words and Music by Teiichi Okano

SUMMERTIME
from PORGY AND BESS®

Music and Lyrics by George Gershwin,
DuBose and Dorothy Heyward and Ira Gershwin

ODE TO JOY

By Ludwig van Beethoven

SCARBOROUGH FAIR

Traditional English

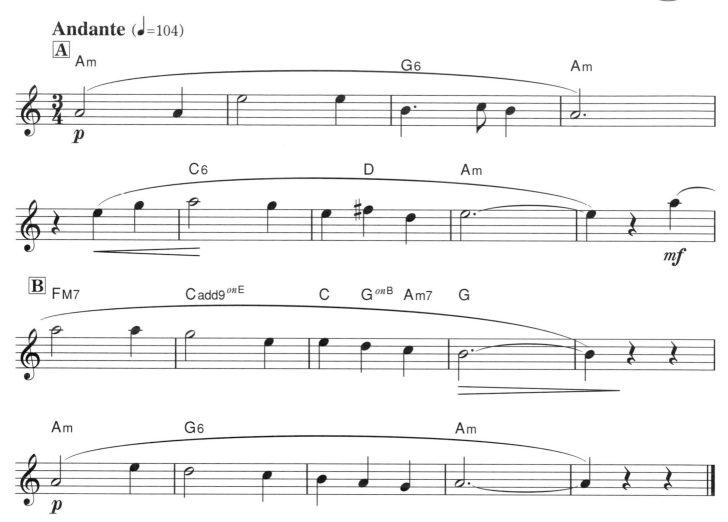

EDELWEISS
from THE SOUND OF MUSIC

Lyrics by Oscar Hammerstein II
Music by Richard Rodgers

JE TE VEUX

By Erik Satie

SOME DAY MY PRINCE WILL COME
from SNOW WHITE AND THE SEVEN DWARFS

Words by Larry Morey
Music by Frank Churchill

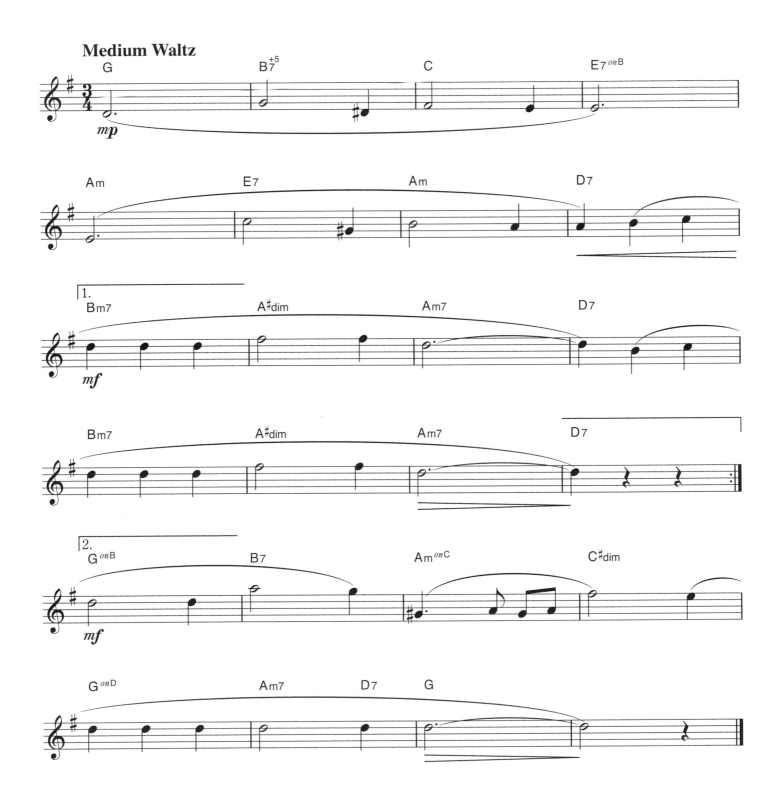

LITTLE BROWN JUG

Words and Music by Joseph E. Winner

SILENT NIGHT

Words by Joseph Mohr
Translated by John F. Young
Music by Franz X. Gruber

MICKEY MOUSE MARCH
from THE MICKEY MOUSE CLUB

Words and Music by Jimmie Dodd

HAMABE NO UTA

Words and Music by Tamezo Narita

MOONLIGHT SERENADE

Words by Mitchell Parish
Music by Glenn Miller

LONDONDERRY AIR

Traditional

MY NEIGHBOUR TOTORO

By Joe Hisaishi

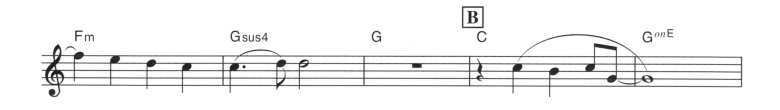

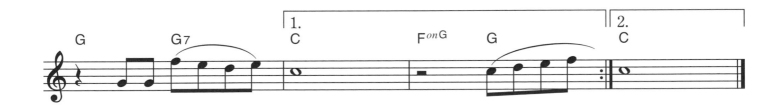

PRINCESS MONONOKE

By Joe Hisaishi

SPRING
from THE FOUR SEASONS

By Antonio Vivaldi

HEIGH-HO

The Dwarfs' Marching Song from SNOW WHITE AND THE SEVEN DWARFS

Words by Larry Morey
Music by Frank Churchill

O CHRISTMAS TREE [DUO]

Traditional German Carol

JOY TO THE WORLD [DUO]

Words by Isaac Watts
Music by George Frideric Handel
Adapted by Lowell Mason
Arr. by Naoyuki Takano

*For solo performance, play the line indicated by the arrow.

EINE KLEINE NACHTMUSIK, K. 525 [TRIO]

By Wolfgang Amadeus Mozart

Arr. by Naoyuki Takano

FINGERING CHARTS

THE GERMAN SYSTEM

Place the tone hole adaptor A (installed at the factory) to set the instrument to the German System fingering.

Semitones such as F#, G# and B♭ tend to easily play sharp, and don't resonate easily. Use fingering, airflow, and embouchure control to adjust intonation.

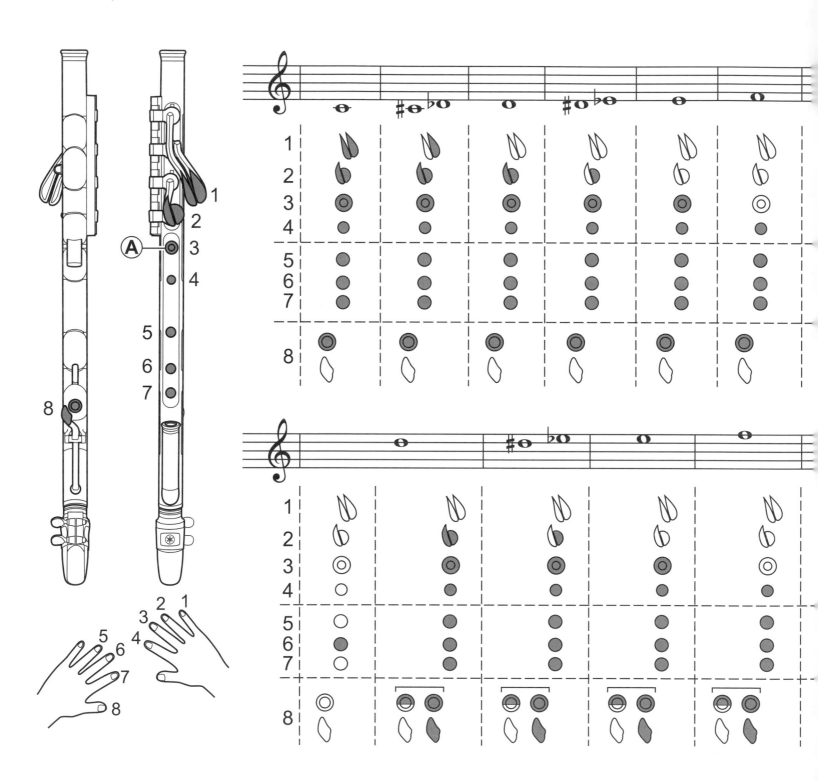

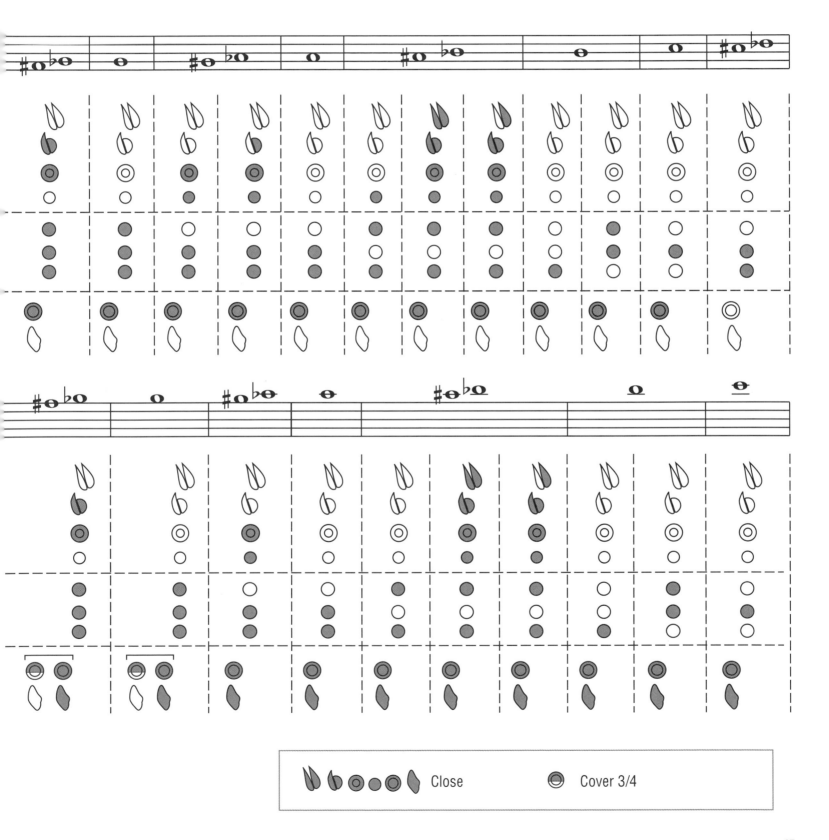

Close · Cover 3/4

THE BAROQUE SYSTEM

Remove the tone hole adaptor A to set the instrument to the Baroque System fingering.

Semitones such as F#, G# and B♭ tend to easily play sharp, and don't resonate easily. Use fingering, airflow, and embouchure control to adjust intonation.

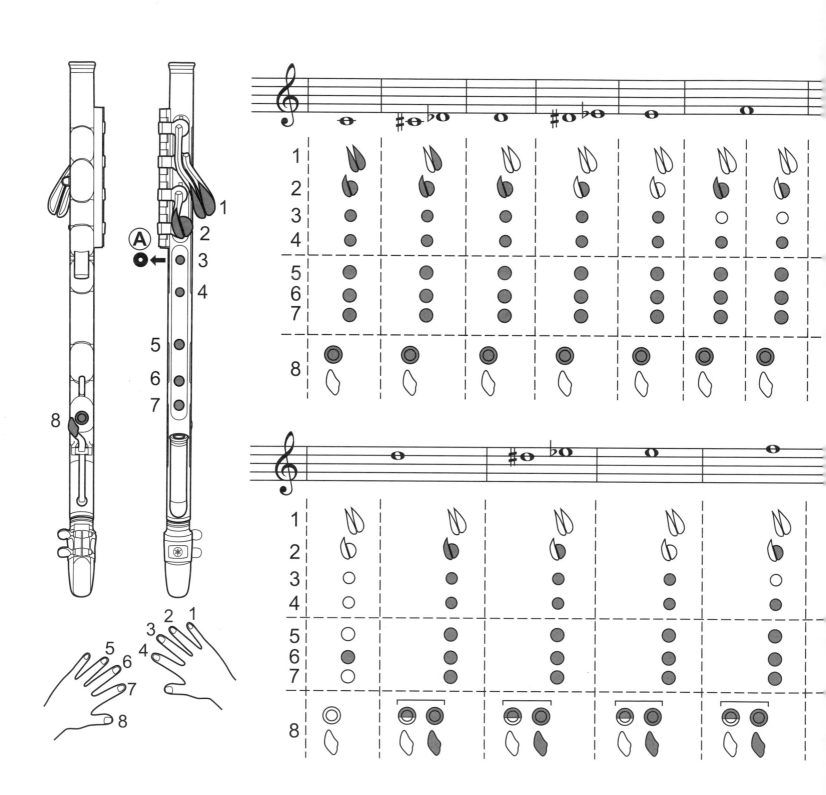

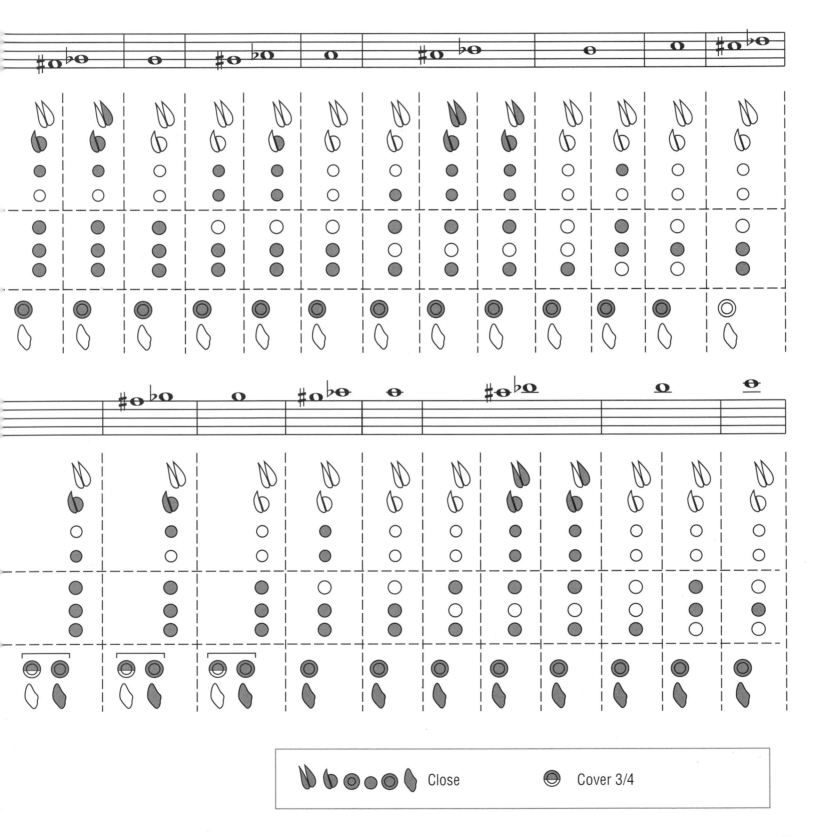

Close | Cover 3/4